ORIOLE PARK BRANCH
7454 W. BALMORAL AVE.
CHICAGO, IL 60656

DISCARD

748

DATE	ISSUED TO
OCT 2 4 1998	
APR 0 5 1999	
MAY 1 7 1999	
MAY 2 2 1999	
AUG 1 1 1999	
JUL 2 2 2004	
AUG 1 9 2004	
DEC 1 3 2004	
JUL 2 0 2005	
AUG 0 8 2005	
SEP 1 2 2005	

UPI 210-3305   Printed in USA

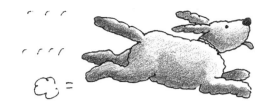

BECOMING YOUR DOG'S BEST FRIEND

BECOMING YOUR DOG'S BEST FRIEND

BY BILL GUTMAN

ILLUSTRATED BY
ANNE CANEVARI GREEN

Pet Friends
The Millbrook Press
Brookfield, Connecticut

Published by The Millbrook Press, Inc.
2 Old New Milford Road
Brookfield, Connecticut 06804

Printed in the United States of America
5 4 3 2

Library of Congress Cataloging-in-Publication Data
Gutman, Bill.
Becoming your dog's best friend/by Bill Gutman:
illustrated by Anne Canevari Green.
p.   cm.—(Pet friends)
Includes bibliographical references (p.   ) and index.
Summary: Provides information about the physical and psychological
needs of dogs, as well as how to choose and
care for them as pets.
ISBN 1-56294-661-7 (lib. bdg.)
1. Dogs—Juvenile literature. 2. Dogs—Behavior—Juvenile
literature. [1. Dogs.] I. Green, Anne Canevari, ill.   II. Title.
III. Series: Gutman, Bill. Pet friends.
SF426.5.G87 1996
636.7'0887—dc20   96-5190 CIP AC

The author would like to thank

Dr. Alan Peterson, DVM,

of Community Animal Hospital
in Poughkeepsie, New York,
for his careful reading of
the manuscript and his many
helpful comments and suggestions.

UNDERSTANDING YOUR PETS

Animals have always played a major role in people's lives. In earlier days, animals did a great deal of work. Oxen pulled the plows that tilled the fields. Horses provided transportation. Dogs were used to guard people and herds of cattle or flocks of sheep. Wherever there were humans, there were usually animals, too.

Today, animals are still a big part of many people's lives. Some still work. Others are kept in zoos or on game farms. And countless millions of animals are simply family pets.

There is much more to pet care than simple feeding and housing. Whether you have a dog, a cat, a bird, tropical fish, a hamster, a gerbil, a guinea pig, or even a horse or pony, you owe it to that animal to learn all you can about it. Obviously, animals can't tell you their feelings. You have to guess what they are thinking and feeling by the way they are acting—by their sounds, their movements, and by changes in their behavior.

This is very important if you want to have a happy, healthy pet that will live out its natural life span. The *Pet Friends* series will not only discuss basic animal care. It will also strive to show what your pet thinks and feels as it lives its life with you.

YOUR PET DOG

In many homes around the world, pet dogs are a real part of the family. They spend nearly all their lives around family members. They wait patiently at the door for a favorite family member to return. Many sleep in their owners' beds. They go with the family on vacations. They love riding in the car and seeing new sights.

Family dogs have even performed heroic acts. Dogs have rescued children from drowning. They have alerted their families to fire in the home. They have frightened off intruders. In many ways they have added to the reasons that dogs have long been called "man's best friend."

Unfortunately, not all dogs are given the chance to provide their families with love and loyalty while enjoying their own lives at the same time. Some people leave the "family dog" tied out in the backyard for hours on end. Others keep their dogs alone in the house all day long. These dogs pine away for companionship and yearn to run and exercise and play with their family or other dogs. Solitary, neglected dogs often become mistrustful, mean, and aggressive.

Other dogs find themselves unwanted by their sheer numbers. Overbreeding and the lack of knowledge about spaying and neutering have left us with too many unwanted dogs. These unfortunate animals languish in dog pounds and must often be put to sleep because no one wants them.

Becoming Your Dog's Best Friend can't really deal with these sad situations. But we hope it will help dog owners to understand their animals better. For example, why is a dog that is left alone miserable? It isn't just that the dog is a friendly animal. Like their wolf ancestors, dogs are social beings. They instinctively *need* to be members of a pack. They need to have physical contact with others they consider part of that pack. Most dogs need a leader that they can follow and please (while some dogs are naturally the leaders).

The pack, or family, stays together. In the wild it would hunt for food together, protect its members from enemies, and raise families. A domestic dog still has the same needs. Without a wild pack to live with, it looks to its new family to be its "pack."

Our pet dogs have many other behaviors that carry over from their days in the wild to life in a human household. It's important to understand the animal's psychological needs as well as its physical ones. Many of your dog's movements—its body language—have special meanings all their own. Butch is not just being cute, playful, good, or bad. He may be trying to tell you something.

Having a well-adjusted, well-behaved, and happy dog is a wonderful experience. One of the most eloquent tributes to a dog was written in 1870 by Senator George Vest, after the death of his loyal canine companion, Old Drum. The tribute said, in part:

"The one absolutely unselfish friend that a man can have in this selfish world, the one that never deserts him and the one that never proves ungrateful or treacherous, is his dog."

WHERE DID MY DOG COME FROM?

Of all the creatures in the animal kingdom, dogs have been friends of people for the longest time. It is thought that dogs have been in the company of humans for about 10,000 years. The modern dog probably originated about 15 million years ago.

Dogs are members of the Canidae family of animals. Also in that family, and closely related to dogs, are wolves, jackals, and foxes. These animals probably evolved slowly from a small tree-climbing, carnivorous (flesh-eating) mammal called *Miacis* that lived 40 million years ago. Believe it or not, it is thought that bears and raccoons also descended from *Miacis*.

The first dogs were wolflike creatures called *Tomarctus*. Some breeds of dogs today (the German shepherd and Siberian husky, for example) are still wolflike in appearance. By studying wolves in the wild, scientists have learned a great deal about dog behavior and needs.

It is thought that early wild dogs were not as fearful of people as the wolf is today. Dogs may have begun coming near campsites and villages to feed on discarded food. Soon the less aggressive dogs were allowed into the camps and villages. The more vicious ones were driven off or killed.

That was the beginning of domestication. A domesticated animal is one that has been tamed to live with people. Early humans began to depend on the dog to warn them of approaching danger. The dog, in turn, began depending on people for food and shelter. It became a mutual bond. Each needed the other in some way.

Very slowly, over hundreds and hundreds of years, dogs became a creation of people. They began to be bred for certain traits. Crossbreeding resulted in new breeds and then more new breeds. That's why there are so many different shapes and sizes of dog breeds today—from the huge Great Dane and Saint Bernard to the tiny Chihuahua and teacup Yorkshire terrier.

Some dogs are still bred for a purpose. They continue to work alongside people or serve as a partner for sporting activities. Others are pampered as household pets.

As we learn more about our pets and why they act as they do, we'll see that much of their behavior continues to relate to the wild. Domestic dogs can still be our best friends, while at the same time retaining traits from the wild that were formed thousands of years ago.

WHAT KIND OF DOG SHOULD I GET?

Your family suddenly decides that it wants to get a dog. So everyone jumps in the car and goes to the nearest pet shop or pound. All of you walk by the cages, looking at puppies. One catches your eye. Everyone agrees. That's the puppy you want.

15

You ask a few questions about it. The clerk isn't too sure what the breed is like, but says it's a great, friendly puppy. So you look no further. You take it home to start its new life.

Six months later your "puppy" has gained 60 pounds (27 kilograms). Your parents don't like the way it sheds hair all over the house and jumps up on everyone, leaving dirty paw prints. The mailman complains that it chases him down the road, nipping at his feet. Finally, your parents suggest that you tie it to a doghouse in the backyard. By that time you're busy with basketball and your friends, so you shrug and say okay.

This kind of story happens too often to families who start out sincerely wanting a dog. The mistake they make is acting too quickly. Yes, lots of people want a dog, but there are many things to consider. You must first think about your own lives and the kind of life you can give to the dog.

How big is your house or apartment? Do you have a yard where a dog can run? Is there someone home most of the time? Can you take the dog with you when you go away? If not, is there someone to take care of the dog?

And what will this kind of puppy be like when it grows up? How big will it get to be? Does it shed hair a lot? Is it the kind of dog that needs constant exercise? Does it drool? Is it a breed that is good with young children? Who in the family will take the responsibility of walking it, feeding it, training it, taking it to the veterinarian? And, maybe the most important thing of all: Why do you really want this dog?

Before you bring a new dog home, there are quite a number of things to consider. Because if you make a mistake, you will make the dog unhappy and your family unhappy at the same time. And the result of a mistake usually means that the dog has to go elsewhere or that it will live a lonely and solitary life.

PURE OR MIXED BREED

The American Kennel Club (AKC), which was organized in 1884, is the largest registration organization for purebred dogs in the world. The AKC now recognizes 138 different purebred dogs. Some breeds, of course, are much more popular than others.

A purebred, however, is not the only option. A mixed breed, mongrel, or mutt, as it is also called, can make a great family dog. Mixed breeds are the result of two or more purebreds being mixed. Some mixed breeds have come from several generations of mixes. So there can be three or four breeds mixed into one. This kind of dog has often been called the All-American Mutt.

There are also those who feel that some mixed breeds are actually hardier and healthier than purebreds. That depends on the dog. The point is that you can get a mixed breed that makes a great family pet. How do you decide?

Even those who think about how a dog will fit into the family situation might not think about the dog. It's just as important to consider the dog's needs as the family's needs. Put those two things together and you probably will make the right choice.

Though mixed breeds often make great pets, it is sometimes easier to predict what a purebred dog will be like. For instance, when considering a purebred, you can read books and talk to experienced breeders about the personality traits of a particular breed (called its *temperament*).

With some mixed breeds, you may have to guess what the temperament will be like, especially if several breeds are mixed into one. However, it is also safe to say that most dogs are looking for love and affection.

ABOUT THE BREEDS

There are many books at libraries and in bookstores that describe all the different breeds of dogs. You can see pictures of the dogs, learn how big they will get, and what some of their basic needs are.

Some larger breeds, such as retrievers, need a great deal of exercise and may not be happy confined to a small apartment all day. Some toy breeds, such as Chihuahuas and some terriers, look cute and cuddly, but are sometimes not dependable around children. They often can't tolerate rough play and can get nippy.

When looking for the right dog be sure to pay attention to the dog's size, the amount of exercise it will need, the kind of grooming you will have to do, and the dog's temperament. Once you pick out some breeds you like, talk to breeders or other people who own that kind of dog. This is an important decision and should not be made hastily.

Many dogs today are still used as workers. Ranch and farm dogs, police dogs, and guide dogs are examples. These dogs are trained with love and kindness. They want to do their jobs well, to please their handlers and owners. Your pet may not have such serious responsibilities, but it will want to please you in the same way. For this, you must do your part as well. And that begins by picking the right dog for you.

ARE YOU REALLY THE DOG FOR ME?

There are certain things you must look for, even before you pick out your new dog. A puppy must be socialized correctly for it to be well adjusted when you bring it home. Socialization is the process of learning how to act with people and other dogs. This is very important, especially in the first twelve weeks of the puppy's life.

Puppies are born with the instincts they would need if they were to live in the wild. If a puppy is raised in a field or woods with no human contact, it will become almost completely untrainable by fourteen weeks of age. It will fear both humans and other animals.

But if a puppy has been socialized during its first weeks of life, it will be relaxed and friendly with the members of its new family. And the puppy will become attached to them much more quickly.

You can find a new dog in several different ways.

PRIVATE BREEDERS

This is the best way to find a well-socialized, well-adjusted pup. Most private breeders take great care with their puppies. They love the parents and make sure each pup in each litter is well socialized.

You will usually find very outgoing, friendly puppies when you visit a private breeder. Most of them will end up being great family pets. A puppy from a private breeder will not be inexpensive. But it will usually be money well spent.

POUNDS AND ADOPTION CENTERS

Pounds and adoption centers serve a wonderful purpose. They find homes for unwanted dogs that have been turned in or abandoned by their owners. Sometimes these places also have puppies. Many times you can get a dog or puppy for just a small donation, so it won't cost your parents too much money.

On the other hand, you often won't know where the puppies came from or how well they have been socialized. Sometimes puppies are abandoned or born outside. If you get a puppy from a pound or adoption center, be prepared to spend a lot of time with the pup. You may have to work hard to get it to lose its shyness and fear. If it doesn't, you will have to treat it especially gently.

PET SHOPS

Puppies in pet shops are often shipped in from great distances. This can cause stress, and sometimes even illness, for the puppy. Sometimes the trauma the puppy suffers during shipping is so great that it is left with a fear of being confined (or even of riding in a car).

Always ask the age of a pup. Also ask how long it has been in the store and how often it has been handled. In some instances a puppy has seen thousands of people through a glass-fronted cage, but if it has been touched by very few, it still has not been properly socialized.

The puppy may seem playful and normal in the cage, but outside it may be shy and fearful. It can be touch-shy or become too excited when handled. Many puppies will get over this, but the more timid ones might never recover completely.

In addition, pet shops often charge more money for a puppy than even local breeders: Your parents may be paying a great deal of money for a poorly socialized pup.

BRINGING THE PUPPY HOME

You can't explain to an animal that it is going to a loving, happy home and that it has nothing to fear. Any new situation will stress an animal, especially a young one. You must allow the animal to relax, then gain its confidence. It has to know from its own experience that you aren't going to hurt it.

For that reason, don't overwhelm your new pet with attention. Don't let all your friends come over and handle it. They may mean well, but too much attention can scare a puppy. It's better to let the puppy explore its new home slowly. If it comes to you, talk to it quietly and pet it. No rough play at first. And don't chase it.

A six- or eight-week-old puppy is still a baby. It needs a lot of sleep and a regular schedule. If the puppy curls up and wants to sleep, let it. Don't wake it up so you and your friends can play with it.

And don't take a new puppy where it can be frightened. A short ride in the car is fine. Meeting new people and other dogs (unless they are bullies or biters) is also good. But a fireworks display or a loud parade could frighten the puppy and make it fearful every time it leaves the house.

You also can't expect a new puppy to be housebroken immediately: It is going to have accidents. Some dogs can be housebroken more quickly than others. Some breeds and individuals
seem to learn in a matter of days; others can take months.

Your new puppy may also chew on something it shouldn't.
Don't discipline it too harshly at first. Be firm in saying "No," but
don't hit it. You may lose the puppy's trust and frighten it. Go
slowly until it is comfortable in its new home.

BEDTIME

There are some pros and cons about where to let your puppy sleep at night. Before you decide, remember this: A dog or puppy is a social animal that would always stay with its pack in the wild. Now you and your family are its pack. Your dog will eventually look at you as the pack leader. Guess where, then, it wants to sleep?

Many people feel the family dog should be locked in a separate room at night. Some put dogs in the basement. Others make it stay outside in a doghouse. It is the firm opinion here that none of these dogs are happy in any situation where they are left alone, even if it's only for the nighttime hours.

Obviously, your dog will be happier and more secure if it is allowed to sleep near you or at least to have access to your room. If it is put by itself for the night, it will not only be unhappy and lonely but will also feel that it cannot protect you. It may even whine or cry at night.

If you don't want your dog on the bed (maybe the dog is too large or is a heavy shedder), why not give it a place in the corner of your room or alongside the bed? That way, the dog will feel secure that it is with you and that it can alert you to any danger.

If there is a special reason why your dog must spend a lot of time outdoors, make sure it has the proper kind of doghouse. A good doghouse should have a raised floor so that no moisture can get in. It should be protected from the wind and be twice the length of the grown dog. The doorway should be covered with a baffle or canvas flap, and the doghouse should not be in the hot sun all day long.

WHAT ABOUT AN OLDER DOG?

Even if your new dog is not a puppy, most of the same rules apply. Let the older dog explore its new surroundings on its own. Don't overwhelm it at the beginning, and don't discipline it immediately. Chances are that an adult dog will be somewhat trained and already housebroken. But it still may have some accidents until it learns its new routine and, most important, learns where the door is.

You won't know much about an older dog. You may not even know the reason its previous owner didn't want it. Any dog, however, will be looking for love and security. Providing that is up to you.

A WORD ABOUT BATHS

When you get a new puppy or even an older dog, your first impulse may be to bathe it. Just a word of caution: Dogs do not need baths very often. Too many baths can cause dry, irritated skin. Of course, a shampoo is necessary if your dog rolls in mud

or gets another kind of dirt on it. Use only a gentle shampoo specially made for puppies or dogs. Otherwise, brushing and grooming will keep it clean without baths.

If you do bathe your dog, especially if it's a puppy, make sure to dry it completely before allowing it out in chilly or windy weather. In the summer, the dog can go outside to dry off.

HOW DO I GET A
MEAL AROUND HERE?

Hundreds of years ago, most dogs, even pets, stayed out in the rain or snow, trotted alongside horse-drawn wagons, slept on the cold, damp ground, and eagerly ate whatever few scraps of left-over food were thrown to them. They fended for themselves.

It's a different world today. There is a whole industry built up around pet care and pet food. And owners are responsible for providing their pet dogs with food, shelter, and a good life.

FOOD SHOULD BE EASY

How do dogs eat in the wild? They are mainly hunters that catch, kill, and eat their prey. Wild dogs or wolves will hunt antelope, bison, deer, and other herd animals. The dogs hunt in packs and generally go after young or weak animals because they are most easily caught. But that doesn't mean dogs eat just meat. This is a common misconception.

Like other living things, dogs in the wild must eat a balanced diet. They do that by eating many parts of their prey: the flesh

31

for protein and fat, and the stomach contents of their kill for grains and vegetable matter. In addition, dogs will crush the bones for calcium and other minerals.

In the wild, a dog's instincts enable it to eat right (providing there is game to be hunted). In your home, giving your dog the right food is up to you. You cannot simply feed a dog meat and think that's enough.

Today, many commercial dog foods on the market are balanced meals by themselves. You can purchase a dry food in the form of kibble, semi-moist food in packages, or moist food in cans. Many vets and nutritionists prefer the dry food because it gives the dog more chewing exercise. That helps keep its teeth clean and gums healthy. The dry food can be moistened with a little water.

You can mix a bit of moist food with the dry for variety. You can also add table scraps, as long as your dog eats its kibble as well. Don't let it become spoiled and just eat "people" food. Dog biscuits are good for treats. They are a balanced food and also help to keep the dog's teeth free of tartar. But don't feed so many treats that your dog won't eat its regular meal.

If you want to give your dog a real bone as a treat, make sure it is a solid, knuckle-type bone. Never give it chicken bones, rib, or chop bones. These can all splinter and cause damage to the dog's stomach and intestines. Some veterinarians feel that giving a dog a real bone is taking an unnecessary risk. There are plenty of other things a dog can chew.

Also, don't be alarmed if your dog bolts its food in huge gulps, acting as if it hasn't eaten in weeks. This is an instinct from the wild. Dogs and wolves often have to eat as fast as they can. They may be competing for the food with five or six others. Or they may sense danger nearby. The dog's digestive system is designed for this kind of eating. Bolting food will not usually make it sick. Many pet dogs, especially the larger breeds, prefer to eat this way.

Have fresh water available for your dog at all times. And make doubly sure of this in hot weather.

There are also special dog foods for puppies and for older dogs. Get the food that is right for your dog.

WHY IS MY DOG DOING THAT?

Why did my dog roll in that awful smelly stuff?

What makes my dog spin around ten times before it lies down?

Why does my dog keep scratching at the sofa with its front paws?

What makes my dog eat grass?

Why does my dog keep chasing cars?

These are just some of the questions that new dog owners often ask about their pets. Some behaviors may make it seem as if your dog is being bad. Others make the dog appear as if it is simply acting strange. Yet these are all behaviors that your house pet has acquired from its ancestors over hundreds of years. Each behavior is related to things that dogs have done, and still do, in the wild.

To understand some of these behaviors is to better understand your dog. No matter how long dogs have been human companions, they have never completely lost their instincts from the wild.

The dog rolling in smelly stuff may simply find the scent appealing to him. But in the wild, dogs on the hunt had a reason

for this. They would roll in something with a strong odor to cover their own scent. That way, the animal they were hunting could not pick up their scent and run away. Your dog may not be about to go hunting, but the instinct to roll in different scents still remains.

How about the dog who spins around and around before lying down? It seems to make no sense, but it does. Dogs outdoors in the wild are looking for the wind direction. They will lie down with their nose pointing into the wind. That way, they can catch the scent of any danger that is approaching.

In addition, dogs sleeping outdoors in very cold weather will turn their backs to the wind and curl up in a tight ball. That is the best way for them to stay warm. The instinct of spinning around, even in the house where there is no wind, also comes from that behavior.

The dog scratching on a hard surface that won't budge, like a tight carpet or floor, is simply trying to make a bed. In the wild, dogs scratched at the leaves and twigs until they had everything set the way they wanted. Watch your dog with a loose blanket. It will scratch and claw it, move it around until it is all lumped up. Then the dog will lie down against it. Your dog has made its bed.

Dogs sometimes eat grass for the purpose of vomiting. The dog's stomach might not feel just right. Maybe it ate a bit too much. You take it for a walk, and suddenly it is eating grass as though it's another meal. Don't take the dog back in right away, because it might soon vomit. And chances are that after vomiting it'll be fine once again. Some dogs, however, seem to enjoy eating grass occasionally just for the fun of it.

Car chasing is very dangerous for a dog: Don't let yours do it. Chances are the same dog that chases cars will also chase kids on bicycles, joggers, and other animals such as rabbits and cats. Not all dogs do it, but those that do are just following their instincts for the chase.

This is once again a throwback to days when dogs had to hunt to survive. It's a prey-chasing instinct that could result in a bite to an unsuspecting person. You might try taking your dog to obedience school. But you should also keep it either on a leash, in a fenced yard, or on a rope. Some animals never lose their instinct for the chase. To a dog, this is fun.

These are not the only instincts that dogs have carried over from the wild. They bark and sometimes show their teeth when a stranger approaches your home because they are defending their territory. This is how they would defend their territory in the wild.

If your dog gets a cut or wound in a place it can reach, it will lick at it constantly. This is not only to make it feel better. The dog's instinct is to keep it from becoming infected. By licking it, the dog is taking dead tissue and bacteria (germs) out of the wound. However, too much licking can slow the healing process. If your dog keeps licking its wound day after day, check with your vet to see how to stop it.

A frightened dog will often roll over and urinate. This, too, goes back to its days in the wild. It is a way an animal submits to the dominant animal in the pack. It is saying, "You win, I give up." Your dog may do this if you yell at it because it is bad, or strike it in any way. It may also show the same behavior if it is in a dogfight and is losing.

In the wild, the dominant dog will stop immediately when the other dog submits and urinates. That's what your dog is hoping—that you will stop disciplining it or that the dog it is fighting with will stop biting it.

These are all behaviors from the wild. They can still dominate your dog's life. The more you learn about these and other behaviors, the better you will be able to relate to your dog and make it a happier animal.

BUT I DON'T WANT
TO SIT DOWN!

A wild dog, such as the Cape hunting dog of Africa, is just that—a wild dog. It is a dangerous animal that certainly won't respond to the command of a human. Your family pet is never going to be a wild dog. But unless you train it to some degree, many of its natural instincts and habits could make it an uncontrollable animal.

Fortunately, a dog's natural instincts also make it one of the most trainable of animals. In fact, the dog is perhaps the only animal that doesn't need food rewards to be trained (although food rewards can be used with success). Dogs can be trained because of the way they lived in the pack. Dogs want to have a leader, someone to show the way.

While each pack of dogs or wolves has one leader, the majority of the animals are followers. In most cases, you can easily take on the role of leader, and your dog will want to be the follower. But there are still some basic things you need to know to be a successful trainer.

You must have a regular training schedule. Dogs like routine, but their attention span is limited. Training sessions, therefore, should not be overly long. Limit them to about fifteen minutes.

You can have several short training sessions a day. If you do it right, your dog will actually look forward to them. That's because a dog always wants attention from its special person. Your training sessions should be with just the two of you. That way, your dog will have you all to itself. And don't forget to use lots of praise. Nothing could make your dog happier.

To train well you must be:

1. Consistent—Train the same way every day.

2. Patient—Don't show anger or annoyance.

3. Persistent—Stick to your routine, even if the dog doesn't get it right away.

4. Calm—Speak quietly. Don't lose your temper. Don't suddenly yell at the dog and, above all, don't hit.

5. Firm—Show your dog you mean business. If it is misbehaving, say "No," firmly. When it settles down, continue.

You must use the same command for a behavior each time. Repeat the command if necessary, then make sure you really praise the dog when it gets your command right. Don't make sudden movements or chase your dog. It must not think training is a frisky game. Don't allow it to pull on your pants leg or play-bite on your finger, hand, or leash. That's yet another game.

In other words, you must show the dog that you are the leader. Training sessions are work. But when your dog does well, the praise it gets and the satisfaction you feel will make it all worthwhile for both of you.

GOOD MANNERS AND SAFETY

Before you start training your dog to obey different commands, there are a few things it should already know. The first, of course, is its name. Most dogs learn their names quickly, especially if you name it as soon as you bring it home and you continue to use the name all the time. If you use the dog's name when giving commands, it will know immediately that you are talking to it. "Sit, Sparky!" "Sparky, come!"

Many of these commands can be very important for your dog's health and well-being. For example, a dog should *always* come when called. You may see potential danger approaching,

such as a car or a much larger dog. If your dog comes immediately, you can keep it out of trouble. If not, you might have a bigger problem to handle.

It's also important for your dog to know what "No!" means. "No" is a very valuable command. It shows your dog that you are not happy and want it to stop whatever it is doing. Again, you are playing on the animal's natural instincts. When you say no to your dog it knows you're not pleased, perhaps even angry. Because you are the pack leader, the last thing your dog wants to do is make you unhappy. Thus a firm "No!" should stop it in its tracks.

A well-placed "No!" can be used to stop excessive barking. Or it can be used to stop a large dog from jumping on visitors to greet them.

TRAINING

There are many ways to train a dog. You can probably find a dozen or more different methods. All of them work if trainer and dog are on the same wavelength. You can read about various training methods in books, or ask a professional trainer what method you might use at home.

When you pick a training method you want to use, remember to apply the principles mentioned before. All training methods rely on repetition and praise, so you will have to work with your dog often. None of the accepted training methods use punishment of any kind.

Besides the basic commands (come, sit, stay, heel), there are many other things, including tricks (like rolling over or "speaking"), that you can then teach using whatever methods work best for you.

There are also dog obedience schools where you and your dog work with professional trainers. This is especially good for stubborn dogs, or sometimes very large dogs that are strong and difficult to handle. Here, you will be working in a large group,

44

with many owners and their dogs. Obedience school can be a fun experience for you and very helpful to your dog.

Occasionally, there may be a strong-willed dog that would have been a pack leader if it had been in the wild. These dogs will want to be *your* leader as well and may be the most stubborn to train. But patience and a firm hand will usually win out.

Remember, an obedient dog is a safe dog, and is a much better companion than a wild and unpredictable one.

WHAT'S WRONG WITH MY DOG?

A veterinarian can sometimes be a dog owner's other best friend. Dogs are normally very hardy animals. But if you think there is something wrong with your dog, don't play guessing games. Take it to your veterinarian quickly.

Like other animals, dogs can't talk and tell you what's wrong. So it's up to you to watch for any changes in your dog's behavior or changes in its appetite. These are two common signs that something is wrong.

Most dogs will become less active and will stay quiet when they are sick or injured. In the wild, their instincts take over and they will try to rest until they get better. Of course, a dog has no way of knowing how serious an illness might be.

If a dog doesn't eat one night, that doesn't necessarily mean it is sick. Its stomach might be slightly out of sorts. Or perhaps it nibbled on the wrong thing outdoors. One night off food shouldn't be too alarming.

But watch for a change in eating patterns. That means if your dog always empties its bowl and suddenly it's eating just half of it or less, then there might be something wrong. Or if it is eating,

then vomiting, you should be concerned. Also, not eating and continuing to vomit could indicate a more serious problem than an upset stomach. It's always better to be safe than sorry.

Shivering is another sign that *may* mean illness. Some dogs shiver when frightened or even excited. They can also shiver when they are cold. But in some instances, shivering can be a sign of pain. Dogs will also whine sometimes if they are in pain. Again, they cannot tell you where the pain is. Unless you know for sure (like a broken toenail or a sprained foot), call the vet.

Other signs to watch for are persistent diarrhea or constipation. Also, if you notice the coat has lost its gloss or the eyes have lost their gleam, you should have your dog examined. Runny eyes or a coated tongue can also indicate sickness. Basically, however, it is a change from the normal, lively, active, hungry animal with a lust for life and desire to follow you everywhere that should tell you that a visit to the vet is in order.

PREVENTABLE ILLNESSES

Dogs can get the same kinds of illnesses that afflict people. They can have coughs, heart problems, and cancer. They can get broken bones, have allergies and skin problems. But there are some illnesses that only dogs (and some other animals) can get. Some of these can be prevented by vaccination.

Vaccinations prevent such canine diseases as rabies, distemper, infectious hepatitis, leptospirosis, and parvovirus. Your vet can also give your dog a blood test for heartworm and put your dog on a preventive medicine in areas where there are mosquitoes that might spread the worm larva to dogs. Heartworm is fatal to your dog unless it is treated.

The rabies vaccine is also very important. In fact, in many places the law requires you to have your dog vaccinated against rabies. Rabies is carried by certain wild animals, especially raccoons, skunks, and bats. Your dog can get rabies if it is bitten by a rabid animal, and then it can pass the disease to humans. Unless it is caught early, rabies will kill. It is a very dangerous disease.

Keeping your dog healthy is not difficult. Regular visits to your veterinarian, good food, and exercise are all important. Large breeds must get out and run. Small dogs can get their exercise right in your house or apartment. No matter where you live, dogs should not be allowed to wander. Even well-fed family dogs sometimes revert to their wild instincts to hunt and kill. They will do this especially if they are running loose with several other dogs and form a small pack.

Your dog's mental health is also important. It must be part of the family to have a sense of well-being. It doesn't want to be left alone, not even if it has the world's best doghouse and food, or even another dog as a friend. Your dog's special times and healthiest times are when it is with you.

WHY CAN'T MY DOG HEAR ME ANYMORE?

Your dog has been your best pal for a few years now. It loves running and romping with you and your friends. It comes whenever you call it. It loves jumping up on you and licking your face when you come home from school. You can even remember your dog being there when you were just a toddler—you have known it all your life.

One day you are romping in the yard with your friends. You turn to look for your dog, but it isn't there. It's at the other end of the yard, just lying down and watching. You call it, but it doesn't come right away. You call again, but it just seems to look through you. You tell it that it's a bad dog, then begin waving your arms. Finally, it gets up and begins coming toward you, only it is walking slowly and limping a bit. You wonder if its leg is hurt. So you go over and begin petting it. Now it is wagging its tail and licking your hand. It'll be okay, you think.

That night you tell your parents what happened. They nod and say, "You know, Duke is twelve years old now. That's very old for a dog. He must be slowing down."

You will find it a sad time when your dog grows old. Since dogs don't live as long as people, most dog owners will have to

deal with an old dog sooner or later. It may not be easy to watch your dog lag behind, to know that it can't hear you calling it anymore, to watch it struggle just to get to its feet.

But, remember, it isn't easy for your dog, either. It still wants to follow you everywhere, to run ahead of you and wag its tail until you reach it. It misses the sound of your voice and feels pain in its legs and hips when it stands up. More than ever, an old dog needs you for companionship and care. It doesn't understand why it can't hear, or can't run fast anymore. But it will accept all that, as long as it still has you.

As a rule, large breeds such as Great Danes, German shepherds, and Labrador retrievers begin showing their age sooner than the smaller breeds like Yorkies, dachshunds, or small terriers. But whenever a dog begins to show its age you must try to be understanding. Here are the changes you can expect to see:

1. The dog will not be able to exercise as hard or for as long.

2. It may lose part or all of its hearing.

3. It may lose part or all of its eyesight.

4. It might develop hip problems or arthritis in the legs, making getting up and moving sometimes painful.

5. It may not be able to control its bodily functions and may have accidents in the house.

6. It will not like any change in its routine.

7. It will be more likely to develop an illness.

8. In some cases, an old dog may become confused and may not even greet or react to you in the same way as in the past.

WHAT TO DO

If you have always loved your dog you will already know what to do. Your dog will need patience, a lot of love and attention, and some extra care. It may not want to play with you and your friends as much. Instead, it may just want to sit on its favorite rug or blanket and watch. Spend some extra time with your dog. Pet and hug it. Let it know you still love it.

Make sure your older dog has regular checkups. Beyond that, here are some other things to do for its health and well-being:

1. Don't overfeed an old dog. If anything, cut back on its food or get a dog food made especially for older dogs. Extra weight is not healthy.

2. Don't force it to exercise. If it's trying hard to follow you and you see it panting or coughing, stop, so it will stop. Make the dog rest.

3. Don't get angry if it has an accident in the house or doesn't obey commands it has been obeying for years. An old dog may not be able to help itself.

4. Check your dog often for signs of illness. If you feel any lumps on its body or it shows any symptoms of being out of sorts, take it to the vet.

5. If you see your dog drinking an excessive amount of water, let your vet know.

6. Don't bring a rambunctious puppy into the house and let it bother the older dog. The puppy will want to play; the older dog won't. If you get a new puppy, try to keep it away from the older dog if the puppy is too rough.

Veterinary medicine has come a long way in treating older dogs. But if your dog is in great pain, don't let it suffer. If your vet thinks it is time to put your dog to sleep, listen to this advice. The vet just wants to do what is best for the dog. You should, too.

WE'RE HAVING PUPPIES!

It can be exciting to watch your dog give birth to puppies. Most dogs are good mothers. They will care for the puppies, nurse them, and allow you to hold them. When the puppies are old enough, you may want to keep one and find good homes for the others. Then the mother can go back to being your pet again.

But puppies must be planned carefully. There are far too many unwanted dogs in the world. Many don't have homes and wind up in dog shelters or pounds. And too many must be put to sleep because no one wants them.

If you have a female dog and don't want to breed her, have her spayed by a veterinarian. That way, she will still be a great pet but she won't be able to have puppies. And if you have a male dog, but don't want him to get any female dogs pregnant, have him neutered. He, too, will still be a great pet and less likely to wander.

In fact, some veterinarians feel that spayed and neutered dogs remain healthier and live longer.

Because there are so many unwanted dogs, breeding should not be done for the fun of it. For the most part, only purebred dogs should have puppies. If your family has a purebred female and decides to breed her to a male of the same breed, then there are some things you should know.

Female dogs can breed only twice a year. They come into "heat," or "season," every six months beginning sometime between the ages of six and ten months. When a female is coming into heat she may become restless and even lose her appetite for a few days. She may also bleed slightly for four to seven days.

After that, she is receptive to a male for three to five days. This may vary somewhat. Males are ready to breed at any time and should be brought to the female at the right time. That is a planned breeding.

If you have a female in heat, you may find every stray male dog for miles around at your doorstep. They will catch the scent. So if you don't want to breed an unspayed female, never let her outside alone.

PREPARING FOR PUPPIES

Puppies are born sixty to sixty-six days after the time the mother becomes pregnant. During that period she should be given more food and maybe even a vitamin-mineral supplement for dogs. Her breasts will start filling with milk and become enlarged about the fifth week. At about the sixth or seventh week you will

be able to feel the puppies inside her. Just run your fingers gently over her abdomen. Don't poke or push at it.

The mother may be uncomfortable during pregnancy. She will need a lot of love and affection from you. No roughhousing, just regular exercise at her own pace. She may also have to go out more often to avoid accidents in the house.

About the eighth week you should prepare a whelping bed. This is a box usually made of wood, big enough for the dog to be able to move about freely. It should not be in a drafty area. The bottom can be covered with shredded newspapers or wood shavings. Let the mother-to-be get used to sleeping in it before she gives birth.

HERE COME THE PUPS

When you think the pups are almost ready to be born, make sure an adult is on hand and that you can reach a veterinarian in case there are problems. When your dog is ready to give birth she will begin pacing, sometimes almost frantically. She may whimper, pant, and strain. Try to keep her in the whelping box.

Each puppy will be born in a fetal sac. The mother will bite the sac to remove it. Then she will eat it. This is perfectly normal. She will lick the pup quite vigorously to get it breathing. If the mother is doing her job, just leave her alone. Remember, she is doing something that dogs and wolves have done in the wild for thousands of years. She knows by instinct what to do.

If the mother is having trouble by laboring too long, call a veterinarian. If a pup is partially out, but won't come the rest of the way, you can help by taking a clean towel or cloth and very gently lifting the pup's head from the mother. Don't jerk or pull hard. If you see the paws emerge first, it is a breeched birth and again you might have to help.

For every pup that comes out, there should be a "placenta," or afterbirth, following. If the placenta does not come out after the pup, it is very important to call a veterinarian.

There are some other birthing problems that may arise. Be sure to learn all you can before your dog gives birth at home. And always have a veterinarian a phone call away.

HELPING TO RAISE THE PUPS

During the first few weeks, the mother will do most of the work with the pups. This includes feeding them, washing them, and keeping them clean. Sometime around the third week she will get tired of nursing. If you see the mother vomit some partly digested food for the pups to eat, then you know it's time to start them on soft puppy foods.

Pups are usually weaned (completely eating on their own) at about three to five weeks of age. Once they are weaned, do not let them return to the mother for milk. It is healthier for the mother to let the milk dry up.

By this time you should be socializing the pups, handling them gently and letting them see new people and places. When they are six weeks old you can begin looking for good homes for them. Eight weeks is about the best time to let them go.

You now have the big responsibility of placing your dog's puppies in good homes. Remember, you have taken the time to learn all about your dog. You know what makes it happy and why it does many of the things it does. You wouldn't want one of your dog's pups going to a place where it was alone day after day, or tied to a doghouse in the yard, or punished all the time because people didn't understand it.

Ask questions of the people who want to buy or adopt a pup, and try your best to get the pup the best possible home. Every dog should have a chance for a healthy and happy life.

FIND OUT MORE

Dogs: *A Complete Guide to More Than 200 Breeds*. Philadelphia: Running Press, 1994.

Jameson, Pam, and Tina Hearne. *Responsible Pet Care Series*. Vero Beach, FL: Rourke Publications, 1989.

Kappeler, Markus. *Dogs Wild and Domestic*. Milwaukee: Gareth Stevens, 1991.

McPherson, Mark. *Choosing Your Pet*. Mahwah, NJ: Troll Associates, 1985.

Roach, Margaret J. *I Love You, Charles Henry: Cats and Dogs in My Life*. Corvallis, OR: Maggie Roach & Associates, 1994.

INDEX